Jennifer Lawrence

By Molly Aloian

Crabtree Publishing Company

www.crabtreebooks.com

Crabtree Publishing Company
www.crabtreebooks.com

Author: Molly Aloian
Publishing plan research and development:
Sean Charlebois, Reagan Miller
Crabtree Publishing Company
Coordinating editor: Paul Humphrey
Editors: Kathy Middleton, Gianna Williams
Photo researcher: Gianna Williams
Proofreader: Wendy Scavuzzo
Designer: sprout.uk.com
Series design: Ken Wright
**Production coordinator and
prepress technician:** Michael Golka
Print coordinator: Katherine Berti

Produced for the Crabtree Publishing
Company by Discovery Books

Photographs:
Alamy: @Moviestore Collection Ltd: pages
6, 12, 17, 27: @AF Archive: pages 8, 14;
@Pictorial Press Ltd: pages 18, 19;
@ZUMA Press, Inc: page 21
Corbis: Michael Hurcomb: page 20;
Kurt Krieger: page 25
Everett Collection: Danny Feld/©TBS: Page 10
Getty: Alexandra Wyman/Getty Images
Entertainment: page 9
Keystone: wenn.com: page 15
Photoshot: page 13; @LFI: pages 22, 26
Shutterstock: Helga Esteb: page 1; Joe Seer:
page 5; Jaguar PS: page 24; s_bukley: cover,
pages 7, 28
Wikimedia: @Mingle MediaTV: page 16

Library and Archives Canada Cataloguing in Publication

Aloian, Molly
    Jennifer Lawrence / Molly Aloian.

(Superstars!)
Includes index.
Issued also in electronic formats.
ISBN 978-0-7787-8051-9 (bound).--ISBN 978-0-7787-8056-4 (pbk.)

    1. Lawrence, Jennifer, 1990- --Juvenile literature. 2. Actors--
United States--Biography--Juvenile literature. I. Title. II. Series:
Superstars! (St. Catharines, Ont.)

PN2287.L28948A46 2012   j791.4302'8092   C2012-906379-7

Library of Congress Cataloging-in-Publication Data

Aloian, Molly.
    Jennifer Lawrence / by Molly Aloian.
        pages cm. -- (Superstars!)
    Includes index.
    ISBN 978-0-7787-8051-9 (reinforced library binding : alk. paper) --
ISBN 978-0-7787-8056-4 (pbk. : alk. paper) -- ISBN 978-1-4271-9070-
3 (electronic pdf) -- ISBN 978-1-4271-9124-3 (electronic html)
    1. Lawrence, Jennifer, 1990---Juvenile literature. 2. Actors--United
States--Biography--Juvenile literature. I. Title.

    PN2287.L28948A58 2012
    791.4302'8092--dc23
    [B]
                                                                            2012037927

Crabtree Publishing Company
www.crabtreebooks.com   1-800-387-7650

Printed in the U.S.A./112012/FA20121012

Published in Canada
Crabtree Publishing
616 Welland Ave.
St. Catharines, ON
L2M 5V6

Published in the United States
Crabtree Publishing
PMB 59051
350 Fifth Avenue, 59th Floor
New York, New York 10118

Published in the United Kingdom
Crabtree Publishing
Maritime House
Basin Road North, Hove
BN41 1WR

Published in Australia
Crabtree Publishing
386 Mt. Alexander Rd.
Ascot Vale (Melbourne)
VIC 3032

CONTENTS

Words that are defined in the glossary are in
bold type the first time they appear in the text.

Meet Jennifer Lawrence

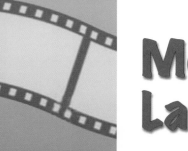

At the age of 21, Jennifer Lawrence became a household name virtually overnight. Playing the role of the **beloved** character Katniss Everdeen in the 2012 blockbuster movie *The Hunger Games*, Jennifer has captivated audiences around the world.

Young Talent

Jennifer has come a long way since her first movie and television roles. Her role as Ree Dolly in the 2010 independent film *Winter's Bone* received much critical **acclaim**. At the age of 20, she was the second-youngest actress ever to be **nominated** for an Academy Award for Best Actress. In fact, *Rolling Stone* magazine has called Jennifer "the most talented young actress in America."

Hard Work Pays Off

Jennifer got her first break in 2007 playing the teenaged daughter of a family counselor in the TV comedy *The Bill Engvall Show*. But superstardom was still a long way off. She worked hard to find movie and television roles that allowed her to showcase her talent as a serious actress. She has come a long way since her small stints in local theater in her hometown of Louisville, Kentucky. Today, her hard work is paying off. Jennifer has brought the bow-and-arrow-toting Katniss Everdeen to life and helped make *The Hunger Games* trilogy the biggest teen movie phenomenon since *Twilight*.

GOOD FRIENDS

Jennifer became good friends with her *Hunger Games* co-star Josh Hutcherson, who played Peeta Mellark. Jennifer and Josh had first met at the Screen Actors Guild (SAG) Awards in 2011.

Jennifer wore a stunning gold gown to the premiere of *The Hunger Games* in Los Angeles, California.

Mystique's mutant power is the ability to "shape shift"—she is able to turn herself into any person.

Feeling Blue

Before *The Hunger Games*, Jennifer was also noticed for her role as the blue, shape-shifting mutant called Mystique in the movie *X-Men: First Class* in 2011. *First Class* is a **prequel** to the rest of the X-Men series. Jennifer's Mystique is a younger version of the character played by Rebecca Romijn in the previous *X-Men* movies.

Popular Attention

Jennifer's movie and television roles have earned her all kinds of awards and nominations, and helped land her on the covers of many entertainment and fashion magazines including *Esquire*, *Flare*, and *Seventeen*. Jennifer uses her newfound popularity to bring attention to various charities and community organizations such as the Bellewood Home for Children. Bellewood is a non-profit agency that helps at-risk and abused children from birth to age 21 across the state of Kentucky.

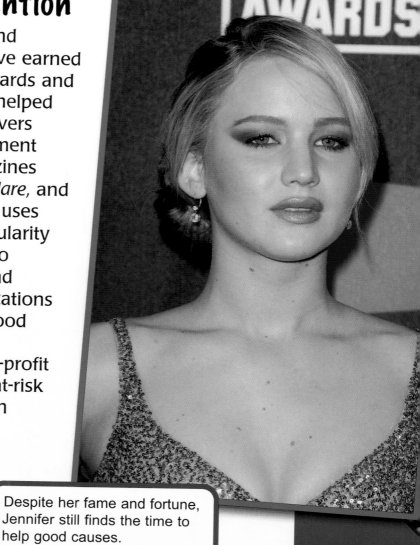

Despite her fame and fortune, Jennifer still finds the time to help good causes.

She Said It

Bellewood is very close to my heart because it's been in my family for generations. My grandfather was Santa Claus during Christmas, my aunt taught horseback riding, my parents, brother, and sister-in-law just opened up our farm at Camp Hi Ho for Bellewood.
—From the YouTube video *Jennifer Lawrence Cares About Bellewood*, 2012

The Early Days

Jennifer Shrader Lawrence was born in Louisville, Kentucky, on August 15, 1990 to parents Karen and Gary Lawrence. Karen runs a children's camp and Gary owns a concrete-contracting business. Jennifer has two older brothers, Ben and Blaine, and a sister-in-law named Meredith. "Jen," as her friends and family call her, was involved in cheerleading, horseback riding, field hockey, softball, and modeling growing up. She first showed off her acting talent in a small role in a church play about the Book of Jonah.

Scouted

When she was 14 years old, Jennifer traveled to New York City with her mom to audition with talent and modeling agencies. While touring around Manhattan, a talent scout asked to take Jennifer's picture. Soon after, agents started to call Jennifer about jobs and appearances, and she began acting in film and television.

With her glowing skin and flowing hair, Jennifer Lawrence looks like the ultimate girl-next-door.

Full Time

Jennifer finished high school early so she could return to New York and begin acting full time. In 2007, she landed a bunch of jobs including an Abercrombie & Fitch ad and a Burger King commercial, as well as appearances in the television shows *Cold Case*, *Monk*, and *Medium*. It was then that Jennifer landed a regular role on *The Bill Engvall Show*. She moved to Los Angeles with her family during the third season of the **sitcom**.

Jennifer poses with her proud parents, Gary and Karen.

She Said It

When I first got to New York, my feet hit the sidewalk and you'd have thought I was born and raised there. I took over that town. None of my friends took me seriously. I came home and announced, 'I'm going to move to New York,' and they were like 'OK.' Then when I did, they kept waiting for me to fail and come back. But I knew I wouldn't. I was like, 'I'll show you.'
—Interview in *The Guardian*, 2010

Young Artist

The Bill Engvall Show was written and created by comedian Bill Engvall. The show was set in suburban Louisville, Colorado. Engvall played a family counselor named Bill Pearson whose own family was experiencing all kinds of ups and downs. Jennifer played Lauren Pearson, his eldest daughter. Jennifer received the Young Artist Award for Outstanding Young Performer in a TV Series for her role in the show. The show ran for three seasons before being canceled in 2009.

COMING UP!

The Young Artist Foundation is a non-profit organization that recognizes excellence in young performers. Jennifer's *The Hunger Games* co-star Josh Hutcherson also won several Young Artist awards for Best Leading Young Actor early in his career.

The Pearson family as they appeared on *The Bill Engvall Show*.

Gaining Independence

At the same time she was appearing as a regular on TV, Jennifer was still pursuing roles in film. She had a string of parts in 2008 that would bring attention to her talent. Besides a small role in the movie *Garden Party*, Jennifer also played a lead character in the drama *The Burning Plain*, opposite actresses Kim Basinger and Charlize Theron. In *The Burning Plain*, Jennifer played a desperate young girl who accidentally commits murder. The movie **premiered** at the 65th Venice Film Festival, where Jennifer won the Marcello Mastroianni Award for Best Young Actress or Actor.

Poker Face

Again in 2008, Jennifer won the lead role in another drama called *The Poker House*, written and directed by actress Lori Petty and based on Petty's own life. Jennifer convincingly portrayed a young girl who is a victim of abuse but who manages to rise above her situation. Jennifer was awarded the Los Angeles Film Festival Award for Outstanding Performance for her role in the movie.

She Said It

Jennifer blew everyone away. There was Jennifer and there was everybody else.

—Lori Petty, *The Poker House* director in a Movieweb interview, 2010

Big Break

Jennifer's next movie role was a **breakout** performance. She portrayed a character named Ree Dolly in the movie *Winter's Bone*. Based on the best-selling novel, the story follows Ree, a 17-year-old girl living in the Ozark Mountains in Missouri. Ree takes care of her mentally ill mother and her younger brother and sister. She soon discovers that her drug-dealing father put the family's home and land up for his **bail bond** before he disappeared and the family now faces **eviction**.

Jennifer liked the *Winter's Bone* script because it wasn't "stupid," like many other roles written for young blondes.

Too Pretty?

When Jennifer auditioned for the part of Ree Dolly, the movie's producers were **wary** of her good looks. They thought Jennifer was too pretty and innocent to play the gritty and resourceful Ree. To Jennifer, the role was an opportunity of a lifetime, and she was determined to get the part.

GOOD FOR A LAUGH

Jennifer Lawrence is known for her down-to-earth personality and quirky sense of humor. The talkative star likes to tell funny stories and joke around in interviews and television appearances. Jennifer even called herself a "troll" during an interview with David Letterman on the *Late Show*.

She Said It

I'd have walked on hot coals to get the part. I thought it was the best female role I'd read—ever. I was so impressed by Ree's **tenacity** *and that she didn't take no for an answer. For the audition, I had to fly on the* **redeye** *to New York and be as ugly as possible. I didn't wash my hair for a week, I had no makeup on. I looked beat up in there. I think I had icicles hanging from my eyebrows.*
—Interview in *The Guardian*, 2010.

Amazing Awards

Jennifer's performance as Ree Dolly greatly impressed audiences, and she received all kinds of **accolades** from directors, producers, and film critics. She received the award for Best Breakthrough Performance from the National Board of Review of Motion Pictures. In January 2011, Jennifer was excited to receive a nomination for the Academy Award for Best Actress. Although she didn't win, she became the second-youngest actress ever to be nominated in that category. She also received nominations from the Golden Globe Awards, Screen Actors Guild (SAG) Awards, Independent Spirit Awards, and the Satellite Awards among others.

Get Crazy!

Jennifer in a scene from *Like Crazy*.

Next up, Jennifer co-starred in the romantic drama *Like Crazy* along with Anton Yelchin, Felicity Jones, and Alex Kingston. The movie tells the story of a college couple facing the challenge of a long-distance relationship. Most of the dialogue in the movie was **improvised**. The movie premiered at the Sundance Film Festival in 2011 and ended up winning the Sundance Film Festival Grand Jury Prize.

Knowing Norah

Coincidentally, Jennifer co-starred again with Anton Yelchin in another movie in 2011. The dark comedy *The Beaver* was directed by Jodie Foster. Mel Gibson plays the part of Walter Black, the depressed **CEO** of a toy company on the brink of **bankruptcy** who begins communicating with a beaver hand puppet. Anton Yelchin plays his oldest son, Porter Black. Jennifer plays the part of Norah, Porter's love interest.

X-posed

In June of 2011, audiences got to see Jennifer in an action role for the first time. Jennifer played the part of scaly blue supervillain Mystique in *X-Men: First Class*. A team of six makeup artists spent seven hours **airbrushing** on the scaly blue **sheath** that made up Mystique's costume. Jennifer had to stand still for seven hours for the makeup and then work a full day on set directly afterward. It was worth it in the end, as *X-Men* fans adored her in the role of Mystique. The film was a huge hit, increasing Jennifer's box-office appeal.

LOVE LIFE

Jennifer Lawrence has been dating the English actor Nicholas Hoult since 2011. The two met in 2010 on the set of *X-Men: First Class*. Nicholas plays the character Hank McCoy—the Beast—in the film. In 2012, Nicholas was named one of *GQ* magazine's most stylish men under 30.

Let the Games Begin!

In 2011, Jennifer Lawrence was well on her way to becoming a superstar. Little did she know that things were about to get crazy. Jennifer was offered the role that would be a total game changer—the part of Katniss Everdeen in *The Hunger Games*. The movie would also star Josh Hutcherson, Liam Hemsworth, Woody Harrelson, Lenny Kravitz, Elizabeth Banks, and Donald Sutherland.

LADY IN RED

Fashion critics deemed Jennifer one of the best-dressed young stars in Hollywood. Twenty-year-old Jennifer Lawrence made quite an entrance at the 83rd Annual Academy Awards on February 27, 2011. She wore a red, figure-hugging Calvin Klein dress with a keyhole back. Fashion fans went crazy for the dress.

Katniss Everdeen wears her dead father's brown leather jacket when she hunts in the forest.

Fight to the Death

The Hunger Games is a science fiction/fantasy story set in a futuristic world in which 12 districts each select one girl and one boy to take part in the **annual** Hunger Games on live television. They are forced to fight to the death until only one remains alive. Katniss Everdeen volunteers to take part in the 74th annual games in place of her sister, Primrose. She trains for the games alongside Josh Hutcherson's character, Peeta Mellark, the boy chosen by her district.

Hello, Heroine

To fans and critics, Katniss Everdeen is a beloved literary character. Jennifer was able to bring this talented, complex, and fascinating heroine to life on the big screen, which is no small feat. It signals a huge shift in the action film **genre**. Such huge blockbuster movies are rarely built entirely around a female action star. Jennifer's role as Katniss quickly turned her into the **highest grossing** action heroine of all time.

She Said It

"I have this feeling of protectiveness over characters I want to play. I worry about them—if someone else gets the part, I'm afraid they won't do it right; they'll make the character a victim or they'll make her a villain or they'll just get it wrong somehow.
—Interview in *W magazine*, September 2010

Best of the Bunch

About 30 actresses auditioned for the role of Katniss Everdeen including Hailee Steinfeld, Abigail Breslin, Emma Roberts, Saoirse Ronan, Chloë Grace Moretz, Jodelle Ferland, Lyndsy Fonseca, and others. *The Hunger Games* director, Gary Ross, described Jennifer as having "an incredible amount of self-assuredness." Despite being a huge fan of the books in the *Hunger Games* trilogy, Jennifer took three days to accept the role of Katniss. Initially, she was a bit intimidated by the size of the production and the possibility of losing her privacy if the series became a huge success. Her desire for the role eventually overcame her fear and she accepted the part.

Jennifer worked long hours to prepare for the role of Katniss Everdeen.

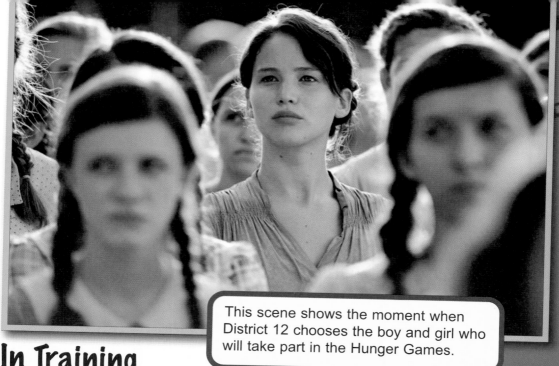

This scene shows the moment when District 12 chooses the boy and girl who will take part in the Hunger Games.

In Training

In the film, Katniss Everdeen is a talented **archer** and an extremely skilled hunter. She had to learn to hunt to keep her family alive in District 12, the coal-mining district that is the poorest and least populated district in Panem. To prepare for the role of Katniss, Jennifer learned archery from an Olympic athlete and also trained extensively in rock and tree climbing, combat, running, and stunt work. She also had to dye her blonde hair brown.

He Said It

"You just got the sense that this 21-year-old girl knew exactly who she was… And then she came in and read for me and just knocked me out… I'd never seen an audition like that in my life. It was one of those things where you just glimpse your whole movie in front of you.

—Gary Ross, *The Hunger Games* director, on Jennifer's audition, interview with Fxguide, 2011

Record-Breaking Release

The Hunger Games was released around the world on March 23, 2012, and set new records for ticket sales. The movie made more than $251 million during its first ten days at the box office. The movie and its stars have won all kinds of entertainment awards. For example, *The Hunger Games* won four awards at the 2012 MTV Movie Awards, including Best Fight and Best On-Screen Transformation. Jennifer won the award for Best Female Performance at the 2012 MTV Movie Awards and her *Hunger Games* co-star Josh Hutcherson won the award for Best Male Performance. The movie also won four Teen Choice Awards.

AWESOME AUTHOR

In March 2012, Amazon announced that Suzanne Collins, the author of *The Hunger Games*, had become the bestselling Kindle author of all time. The first book in the trilogy was published in 2008. The print versions of the books have sold more than 23 million copies.

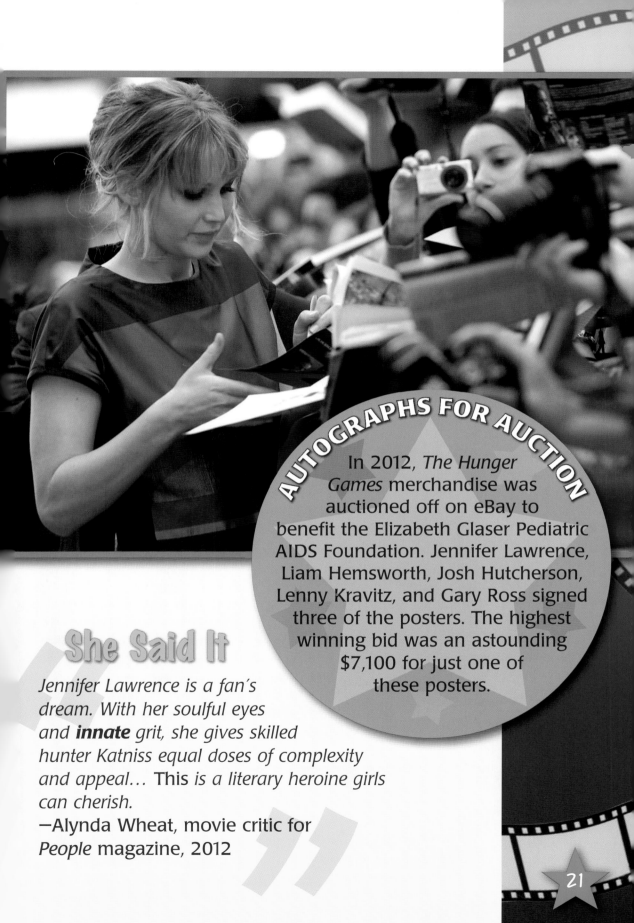

AUTOGRAPHS FOR AUCTION

In 2012, *The Hunger Games* merchandise was auctioned off on eBay to benefit the Elizabeth Glaser Pediatric AIDS Foundation. Jennifer Lawrence, Liam Hemsworth, Josh Hutcherson, Lenny Kravitz, and Gary Ross signed three of the posters. The highest winning bid was an astounding $7,100 for just one of these posters.

She Said It

*Jennifer Lawrence is a fan's dream. With her soulful eyes and **innate** grit, she gives skilled hunter Katniss equal doses of complexity and appeal... **This** is a literary heroine girls can cherish.*
—Alynda Wheat, movie critic for *People* magazine, 2012

Catching Fire

The next movie in the trilogy, *The Hunger Games: Catching Fire*, is being directed by Francis Lawrence. It is due for release in the fall of 2013. Many of the same actors and actresses, including Jennifer Lawrence, Josh Hutcherson, Liam Hemsworth, Elizabeth Banks, Donald Sutherland, and Woody Harrelson, are featured in the movie, but there are some new stars, too.

Jennifer Lawrence, Josh Hutcherson, and Liam Hemsworth will all star in *The Hunger Games: Catching Fire*.

New Rules

The Hunger Games: Catching Fire continues the story of Katniss Everdeen and her life in Panem. After the events in *The Hunger Games*, a rebellion against the **oppressive** Capitol metropolis that rules Panem has begun, and Katniss and Peeta are forced to return to the arena for the Quarter Quell, a special Hunger Games that occurs every 25 years. Each Quell includes a new twist to the rules in the arena.

FIGHTING HUNGER

In 2012, the lead cast of *The Hunger Games*—Jennifer Lawrence, Josh Hutcherson, and Liam Hemsworth—teamed up with Feeding America to help fight hunger. Feeding America is the country's leading hunger-relief charity and helps provide food to over 37 million Americans each year. The cast lent their voices to a public service announcement for the campaign.

Fans

Fans are obsessed with Katniss Everdeen, and at just 22 years old, Jennifer is now a full-blown international superstar with millions of adoring fans throughout the world. She has thousands of friends on Facebook and thousands of followers on Twitter. Despite all the fame and attention, Jennifer tries to remain true to herself.

She Said It

There are actresses who build themselves, and then there are actresses who are built by others. I want to build myself.

—Interview with *W magazine*, 2012

Hungry for More

Fans are **ravenous** for Jennifer Lawrence! She is quickly becoming one of the most talked about and well-respected young actresses in Hollywood and she shows no signs of slowing down. Jennifer continues to work hard to get challenging, interesting roles that offer audiences a different perspective on what makes a strong female lead. Four feature films starring Jennifer have been released in 2012: *The Hunger Games*, *The Devil You Know*, *House at the End of the Street*, and the *Silver Linings Playbook*.

Mystery Thriller

Jennifer has a very brief appearance in the 2012 mystery thriller *The Devil You Know*. The movie is about a former movie star with a dark secret whose daughter, Zoe Hughes, hopes to become an actress, too. Jennifer plays the younger version of Rosamund Pike's character Zoe Hughes.

Jennifer looked as stunning as ever at the 63rd Annual Directors Guild of America Awards in January 2011.

Trying New Things

Jennifer tried her hand at a new genre in the 2012 horror thriller called *House at the End of the Street*. The movie also stars Elisabeth Shue, Max Thieriot, and Gil Bellows. A fan of horror movies, Jennifer wanted to try being in one because it would take her out of her "comfort zone" as an actress. She said she had fun working on her scream.

Staying Fit and Healthy

Jennifer maintains a healthy lifestyle by working out and eating healthy. She does not diet and has spoken out about the dangers of girls getting carried away with dieting and exercise.

At *The Hunger Games* premiere in Berlin, Germany, Jennifer wore this red "fire dress."

She Said It

I like food. I don't really diet or anything. I'm miserable when I'm dieting and I like the way I look. I'm really sick of all these actresses looking like birds… I'd rather look a little chubby on camera and look like a person in real life, than look great on screen and look like a scarecrow in real life.
—*Flare* magazine interview, 2011

VIDEO STAR

Jennifer appeared in a music video for the song "The Mess I Made" by the American rock band called Parachute from Charlottesville, Virginia. The song was on the band's 2009 album called *Losing Sleep*.

Books to Movies

The film *Silver Linings Playbook* was released in the fall of 2012. Jennifer Lawrence and Bradley Cooper star in the movie. Jennifer was thrilled to get to act with Hollywood heavyweight Robert De Niro who had a supporting role in the film. Adapted from a novel, Jennifer plays a character named Tiffany in this movie about a former teacher who moves back in with his mother after spending four years in a mental health facility.

Jennifer quickly moved on to do another film based on a novel called *Serena*, again starring opposite Bradley Cooper. In a complete reverse from their comic pairing in *Silver Linings Playbook*, they play an ambitious couple in the 1920s timber trade. Her character will stop at nothing to succeed, including murder. This film will be released in 2013.

Jennifer poses with Bradley Cooper at the *Silver Linings Playbook* premiere in Toronto.

She Said It

I don't know if this is why everything has worked so well and I'm not sure I'd recommend this kind of thinking to anyone else, but I've always known I'd be successful in acting. I have certainly worked for it.
—jenniferlawrencedaily.tumblr.com, 2012

Future Past

Jennifer will bring Mystique back to the screen in *X-Men: Days of Future Past* in the summer of 2014. The new *X-Men* film will deal with alternating timelines, with some characters living in the future and others living in the present or past. Her co-stars are James McAvoy and Michael Fassbender.

Glass Castle

It is also rumored that Jennifer will be starring in the upcoming movie *The Glass Castle*. This film is based on the **memoir** of the writer/journalist Jeannette Walls, and Jennifer is in talks about taking on the female lead. In 2005, the book spent more than 250 weeks on the *New York Times* bestsellers list, which was a first for any memoir.

You'll see many of the stars from *X-Men: First Class*, including Jennifer Lawrence, in the next *X-Men* film, due out in 2014.

Jennifer has come a long way since her debut television and movie roles.

Looking to the Future

Jennifer says she is drawn to roles in films that are dark and that have artistic value to them. No doubt she will continue in these kinds of dramatic roles, as well as take on different genres outside her "comfort zone." Having achieved superstardom with the release of *The Hunger Games*, Jennifer continues to deal with the intense interest in her personal life. She has discussed the possibility of moving out of Los Angeles to escape being constantly followed by photographers. But fans have no need to worry. This serious performer is dedicated to her craft and has a long film career ahead of her.

PLAYING FAVORITES

One of Jennifer's favorite male actors is American actor James Franco because he is a "hunk that can act." Cate Blanchett, Meryl Streep, and Laura Linney are some female actresses who have inspired Jennifer.

She Said It

I'd like to direct at some point. But I don't know, because 10 years ago I would have never imagined that I'd be here. So in 10 years from now, I might be running a rodeo.
—Interview in *FLARE* magazine, May 2011

Timeline

1990: Jennifer Shrader Lawrence is born on August 15 in Louisville, Kentucky

2004: She goes to New York City with her mom for auditions with talent and modeling agencies

2006–2008: She appears in episodes of *Monk, Cold Case,* and *Medium*

2007–2009: She lands a spot on the TBS sitcom *The Bill Engvall Show*. She wins a Young Artist Award for her performance on the show

2008: She has a small role in the movie *Garden Party* and appears in the independent movie *The Burning Plain*; she wins the Marcello Mastroianni Award for Best Young Actress or Actor

2008: She lands her first lead role in the movie *The Poker House*; she wins the Los Angeles Film Festival Award for Outstanding Performance

2010: She wows audiences in *Winter's Bone*

2011: She receives a nomination for the Academy Award for Best Actress

2011: She co-stars in the romantic drama *Like Crazy* and the dark comedy *The Beaver*

2011: She plays Mystique in *X-Men: First Class*

2011: On March 11, she is offered the part of Katniss Everdeen in *The Hunger Games*

2012: *The Hunger Games* is released on March 23

2012: She wins the award for Best Female Performance at the 2012 MTV Movie Awards

2012: She stars in the horror thriller *House at the End of the Street*

2012: *The Silver Linings Playbook* is released starring Jennifer Lawrence and Bradley Cooper

2013: *The Hunger Games: Catching Fire* is released with Jennifer resuming her role as Katniss

2013: *Serena* is released, again co-starring Jennifer with Bradley Cooper

2014: Reprising her role as Mystique, *X-Men: Days of Future Past* is due for release in the summer

Glossary

acclaim Public praise

accolades Praise or approval

airbrushing Using compressed air to apply a liquid, such as paint, as a fine spray

annual Something that takes place once every year

archer A person who can use a bow and arrow

bail An amount of money that releases someone from jail while they wait for their trial

bankruptcy When a person can no longer pay his or her debts

beloved Something or someone that is loved dearly

bond A pledge or promise to pay a certain sum on or before a stated day

breakout To become famous or noticed

CEO Stands for Chief Executive Officer. A CEO is the highest ranking person or leader who oversees the management of a business.

eviction To remove people from their property by legal action

genre A type or category of artistic composition

highest grossing A film that earns the most money

improvised Performances that have no written script

innate Describing a quality or ability one is born with

memoir A story about a personal experience

nominated Chosen as a candidate for an award

oppressive Cruel or harsh

premiered Performed or showed for the first time

prequel A film whose story shows the events that happened in the lead-up to a previous film

ravenous Very hungry

redeye A late-night or overnight flight

sheath A type of tight covering

sitcom (short for situation comedy) A television program based on funny situations

tenacity Persistence or stubbornness

wary Very cautious

Find Out More

Books

Gosman, Gillian. *Jennifer Lawrence (Kid Stars!)*. New York: Powerkids Press, 2012.

Krohn, Katherine. *Jennifer Lawrence: Star of the Hunger Games (Gateway Biographies)*. Minneapolis: Lerner Publishing Group, 2012.

O'Shea, Mick. *Beyond District 12: The Stars of the Hunger Games*. London, England: Plexus Publishing, 2012.

Williams, Mel. *Stars in the Arena: Meet the Hotties of* The Hunger Games. New York: Simon Pulse, 2012.

Websites

The Official Website for Jennifer Lawrence
http://jenniferslawrence.com

Jennifer Lawrence Daily
http://jenniferlawrencedaily.com

The Hunger Games by Suzanne Collins
http://www.scholastic.com/thehungergames

Index

About the Author

Molly Aloian has written more than 60 nonfiction books for children on a wide variety of topics, including mountains and rivers, chemistry, holidays and celebrations around the world, animal life cycles, endangered animals, and continents and their geography. When she is not busy writing, she enjoys practicing yoga, traveling, and cooking.